Note to parents

Multiplication is simply a quick method of adding up several numbers of equal size. Once learned, these facts make calculation quicker and easier.

At first, learning these facts should be related to everyday situations at a very simple level. Let your child sort out his or her toys into equal sets e.g. 3 sets of 4 toy cars is 12 cars altogether. Point out that you are adding the same number each time (4 and 4 more and 4 more). Always talk about what you are doing, because understanding comes before memorizing. Look for real-life examples of equal sets and ask your child questions like, "How many wheels on 2 bikes? How many eggs in 3 boxes?" But let him or her count the objects to get the answer in the early stages. The pictures on the right-hand pages provide further examples of equal sets. Much of a child's understanding of mathematics depends very much on the spoken language involved in sorting out the problem.

Children cannot learn all the multiplication facts at once or at the same rate. They need a gradual and thorough building up of knowledge, so present only a few facts at a time. Memorizing the tables can be fun. Say the counting rhymes in this book as you walk down the street together, or use them as skipping rhymes. Making up your own games is often very effective. Above all, learning can and should be enjoyable.

Rhona Whiteford B.A. (Open), Cert. Ed.
Teacher

times tables

written by Rhona Whiteford

illustrated by Jo Wright

Filmset in Nelson Teaching Alphabet
by kind permission of
Thomas Nelson and Sons Ltd.

Copyright © 1989 by World International Publishing Limited.
All rights reserved.
Published in Great Britain by World International Publishing Limited,
An Egmont Company, Egmont House, P.O. Box 111, Great Ducie Street,
Manchester M60 3BL.
Printed in DDR. ISBN 0 7235 2471 8

A CIP catalogue record for this book is available from the British Library

There are **twos** all around.

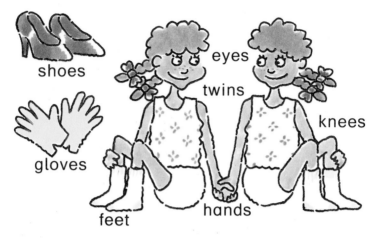

shoes

gloves

feet

eyes

twins

hands

knees

Here is **1** set of **2** mittens.

1 x 2 = 2

Here are **2** sets of **2** mittens.

2 x 2 = 4

If you have **2 x 3**

you have **6** altogether.

If you have **3 x 2**

you still have **6** altogether.

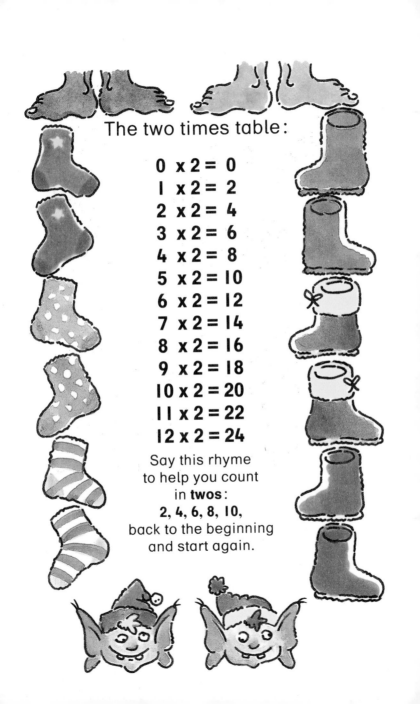

The two times table:

$$0 \times 2 = 0$$
$$1 \times 2 = 2$$
$$2 \times 2 = 4$$
$$3 \times 2 = 6$$
$$4 \times 2 = 8$$
$$5 \times 2 = 10$$
$$6 \times 2 = 12$$
$$7 \times 2 = 14$$
$$8 \times 2 = 16$$
$$9 \times 2 = 18$$
$$10 \times 2 = 20$$
$$11 \times 2 = 22$$
$$12 \times 2 = 24$$

Say this rhyme
to help you count
in **twos**:
2, 4, 6, 8, 10,
back to the beginning
and start again.

There are **threes** all around.

Here is **1** set of **3** traffic-lights.

1 x 3 = 3

Here are **2** sets of **3** traffic-lights.

2 x 3 = 6

If you have **3 x 4**

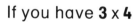

you have **12** altogether.

If you have **4 x 3**

you still have **12** altogether.

The three times table:

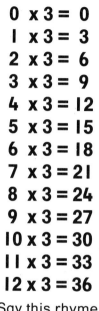

0 x 3 = 0
1 x 3 = 3
2 x 3 = 6
3 x 3 = 9
4 x 3 = 12
5 x 3 = 15
6 x 3 = 18
7 x 3 = 21
8 x 3 = 24
9 x 3 = 27
10 x 3 = 30
11 x 3 = 33
12 x 3 = 36

Say this rhyme
to help you count
in **threes**:
3, 6, 9, 12, 15,
wash your hands
and make them clean.

There are **fours** all around.

Here is **1** set of **4** wheels.

Here are **2** sets of **4** wheels.

1 x 4 = 4

2 x 4 = 8

If you have **4** x **5**

you have **20** altogether.

If you have **5** x **4**

you still have **20** altogether.

The four times table:

$$0 \times 4 = 0$$
$$1 \times 4 = 4$$
$$2 \times 4 = 8$$
$$3 \times 4 = 12$$
$$4 \times 4 = 16$$
$$5 \times 4 = 20$$
$$6 \times 4 = 24$$
$$7 \times 4 = 28$$
$$8 \times 4 = 32$$
$$9 \times 4 = 36$$
$$10 \times 4 = 40$$
$$11 \times 4 = 44$$
$$12 \times 4 = 48$$

Say this rhyme
to help you count
in **fours**:
4, 8, 12, 16,
add **4** each time
– see what I mean?

There are **fives** all around.

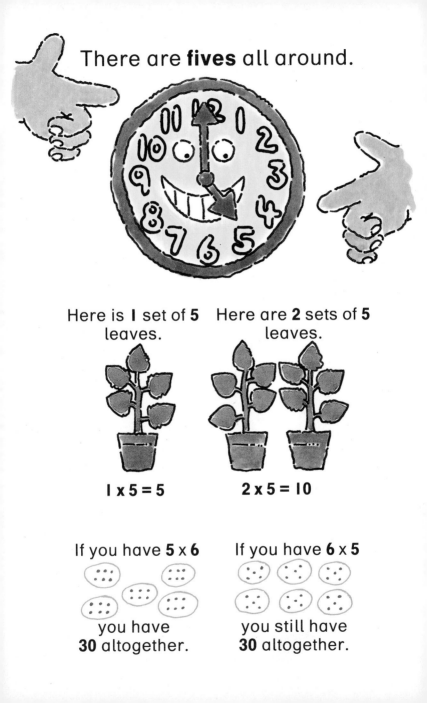

Here is **1** set of **5** leaves.

1 x 5 = 5

Here are **2** sets of **5** leaves.

2 x 5 = 10

If you have **5 x 6** you have **30** altogether.

If you have **6 x 5** you still have **30** altogether.

The five times table:

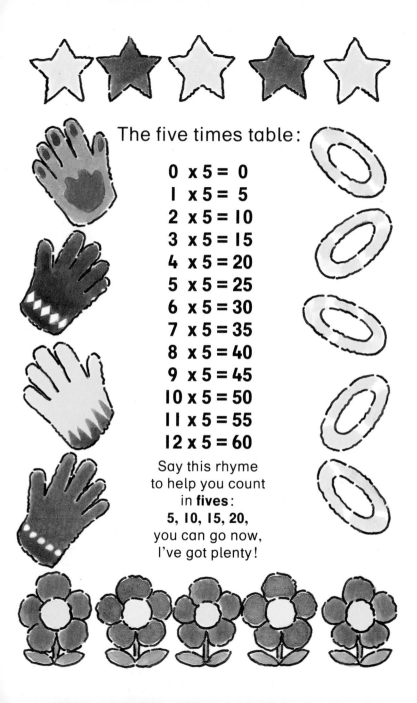

0 x 5 = 0
1 x 5 = 5
2 x 5 = 10
3 x 5 = 15
4 x 5 = 20
5 x 5 = 25
6 x 5 = 30
7 x 5 = 35
8 x 5 = 40
9 x 5 = 45
10 x 5 = 50
11 x 5 = 55
12 x 5 = 60

Say this rhyme
to help you count
in **fives**:
5, 10, 15, 20,
you can go now,
I've got plenty!

There are **sixes** all around.

Here is **1** set of **6** eggs.

Here are **2** sets of **6** eggs.

1 x 6 = 6

2 x 6 = 12

If you have **6 x 3**

you have **18** altogether.

If you have **3 x 6**

you still have **18** altogether.

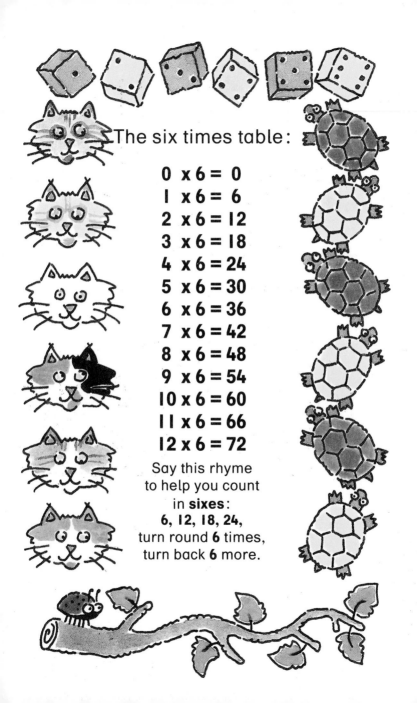

The six times table:

$$0 \times 6 = 0$$
$$1 \times 6 = 6$$
$$2 \times 6 = 12$$
$$3 \times 6 = 18$$
$$4 \times 6 = 24$$
$$5 \times 6 = 30$$
$$6 \times 6 = 36$$
$$7 \times 6 = 42$$
$$8 \times 6 = 48$$
$$9 \times 6 = 54$$
$$10 \times 6 = 60$$
$$11 \times 6 = 66$$
$$12 \times 6 = 72$$

Say this rhyme
to help you count
in **sixes**:
6, 12, 18, 24,
turn round **6** times,
turn back **6** more.

There are **sevens** all around.

MONDAY **1** APRIL	
TUESDAY **2** APRIL	
WEDNESDAY **3** APRIL	
THURSDAY **4** APRIL	
FRIDAY **5** APRIL	
SATURDAY **6** APRIL	
SUNDAY **7** APRIL	

Here is **1** set of **7** buttons.

Here are **2** sets of **7** buttons.

1 x 7 = 7

2 x 7 = 14

If you have **7** x **5**

you have **35** altogether.

If you have **5** x **7**

you still have **35** altogether.

The seven times table:

$0 \times 7 = 0$
$1 \times 7 = 7$
$2 \times 7 = 14$
$3 \times 7 = 21$
$4 \times 7 = 28$
$5 \times 7 = 35$
$6 \times 7 = 42$
$7 \times 7 = 49$
$8 \times 7 = 56$
$9 \times 7 = 63$
$10 \times 7 = 70$
$11 \times 7 = 77$
$12 \times 7 = 84$

Say this rhyme
to help you count
in **sevens**:
7, 14, 21, 28,
3 cats **3** dogs
and **1** frog on a skate.

There are **eights** all around.

Here is **1** set of **8** candles.

$$1 \times 8 = 8$$

Here are **2** sets of **8** candles.

$$2 \times 8 = 16$$

If you have **8 x 4**

you have **32** altogether.

If you have **4 x 8**

you still have **32** altogether.

The eight times table:

0	x 8 =	0
1	x 8 =	8
2	x 8 =	16
3	x 8 =	24
4	x 8 =	32
5	x 8 =	40
6	x 8 =	48
7	x 8 =	56
8	x 8 =	64
9	x 8 =	72
10	x 8 =	80
11	x 8 =	88
12	x 8 =	96

Say this rhyme
to help you count
in **eights**:
8, 16, 24, 32,
keep on adding **8**
– it's not hard to do.

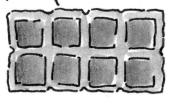

There are **nines** all around.

Here is **1** set of **9** skittles.

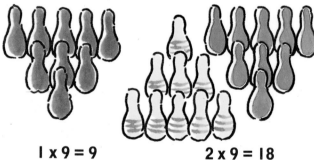

$$1 \times 9 = 9$$

Here are **2** sets of **9** skittles.

$$2 \times 9 = 18$$

If you have **3** x **9**

you have
27 altogether.

If you have **9** x **3**

you still have
27 altogether.

The nine times table:

$0 \times 9 = 0$
$1 \times 9 = 9$
$2 \times 9 = 18$
$3 \times 9 = 27$
$4 \times 9 = 36$
$5 \times 9 = 45$
$6 \times 9 = 54$
$7 \times 9 = 63$
$8 \times 9 = 72$
$9 \times 9 = 81$
$10 \times 9 = 90$
$11 \times 9 = 99$
$12 \times 9 = 108$

Say this rhyme
to help you count
in **nines**:
9, 18, 27, 36,
keep saying this
until it sticks.

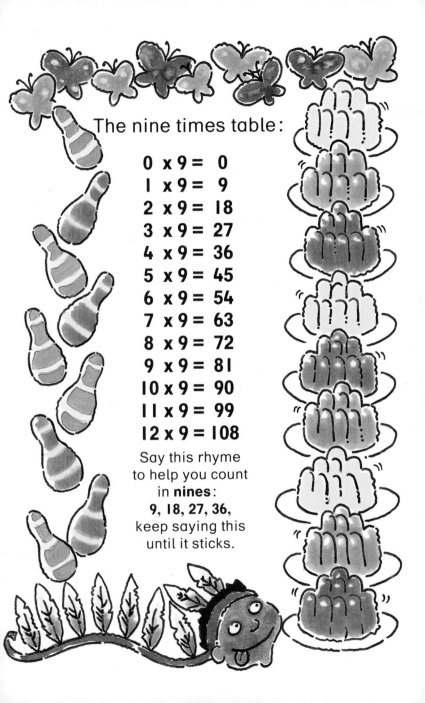

There are **tens** all around.

Here is 1 set of **10** marbles.

1 x 10 = 10

Here are **2** sets of **10** marbles.

2 x 10 = 20

If you have **10 x 1**

you have **10** altogether.

If you have **1 x 10**

you still have **10** altogether.

The ten times table:

$$0 \times 10 = 0$$
$$1 \times 10 = 10$$
$$2 \times 10 = 20$$
$$3 \times 10 = 30$$
$$4 \times 10 = 40$$
$$5 \times 10 = 50$$
$$6 \times 10 = 60$$
$$7 \times 10 = 70$$
$$8 \times 10 = 80$$
$$9 \times 10 = 90$$
$$10 \times 10 = 100$$
$$11 \times 10 = 110$$
$$12 \times 10 = 120$$

Say this rhyme
to help you count
in **tens**:
10, 20, 30, 40,
this is simple
– just add a nought, see!

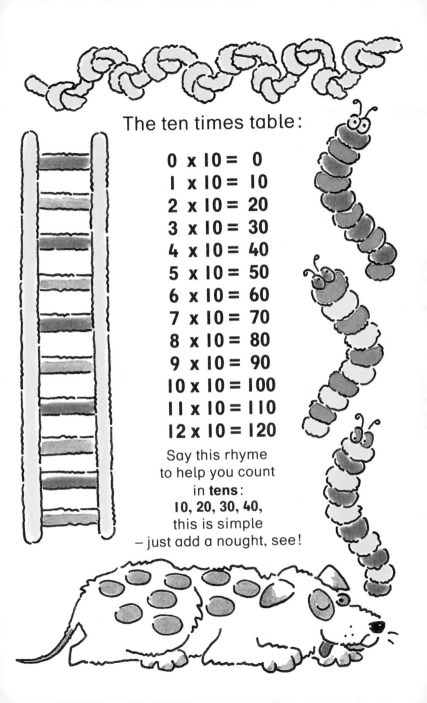

There are **elevens** all around.

Here is **I** set of **I I** sweets.

I x I I = I I

Here are **2** sets of **I I** sweets.

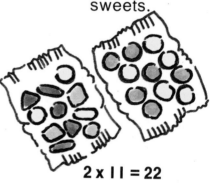

2 x I I = 22

If you have **I I x 2**

you have **22** altogether.

If you have **2 x I I**

you still have **22** altogether.

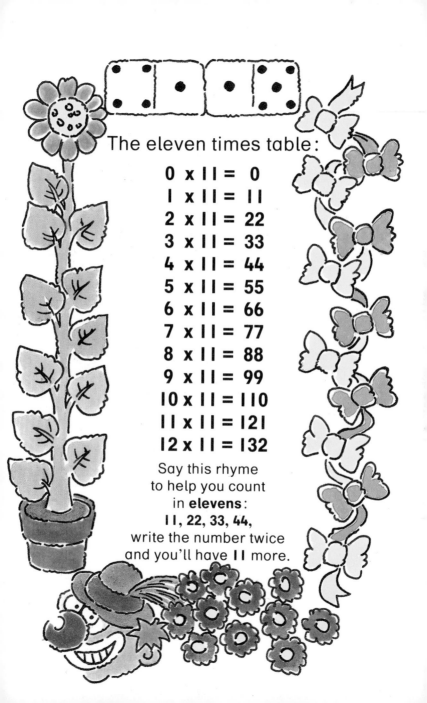

The eleven times table:

0 × 11 =	0
1 × 11 =	11
2 × 11 =	22
3 × 11 =	33
4 × 11 =	44
5 × 11 =	55
6 × 11 =	66
7 × 11 =	77
8 × 11 =	88
9 × 11 =	99
10 × 11 =	110
11 × 11 =	121
12 × 11 =	132

Say this rhyme
to help you count
in **elevens**:
11, 22, 33, 44,
write the number twice
and you'll have **11** more.

There are **twelves** all around.

Here is **1** set of **12** bottles.

$1 \times 12 = 12$

Here are **2** sets of **12** bottles.

$2 \times 12 = 24$

If you have **12 x 3**

you have **36** altogether.

If you have **3 x 12**

you still have **36** altogether.

The twelve times table:

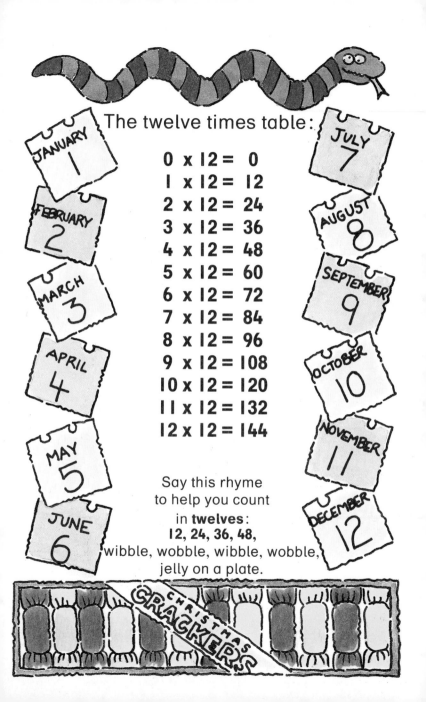

0	x 12 =	0
1	x 12 =	12
2	x 12 =	24
3	x 12 =	36
4	x 12 =	48
5	x 12 =	60
6	x 12 =	72
7	x 12 =	84
8	x 12 =	96
9	x 12 =	108
10	x 12 =	120
11	x 12 =	132
12	x 12 =	144

Say this rhyme
to help you count
in **twelves**:
12, 24, 36, 48,
wibble, wobble, wibble, wobble,
jelly on a plate.

JANUARY 1
FEBRUARY 2
MARCH 3
APRIL 4
MAY 5
JUNE 6
JULY 7
AUGUST 8
SEPTEMBER 9
OCTOBER 10
NOVEMBER 11
DECEMBER 12

Which balloon belongs to which child?

Which tables do you know?

This is to certify that

(name)
_____

knows these tables:

	tick
2 times	
3 times	
4 times	
5 times	
6 times	
7 times	
8 times	
9 times	
10 times	
11 times	
12 times	

signed

_____ parent/guardian

Do you know these facts?